The Science of Living Things

What is a Mammal?

 A Bobbie Kalman Book

Crabtree Publishing Company

The Science of Living Things Series
A Bobbie Kalman Book

For marvelous Meredith

Editor-in-Chief
Bobbie Kalman

Writing team
Bobbie Kalman
Greg Nickles
Niki Walker
Managing editor
Lynda Hale

Editors
Niki Walker
Jacqueline Langille

Text and photo research
Greg Nickles

Computer design
Lynda Hale
McVanel Communications Inc.
  (cover concept)
Nancy Twerdohlib

Production coordinator
Hannelore Sotzek

Consultant
K. Diane Eaton, Hon. B.Sc., B.A.,
Brock University

Special thanks to
Danielle Gentile

Photographs
Gregory G. Dimijian/Photo Researchers, Inc.: page 14
Petrina Gentile: page 7 (top)
Wolfgang Kaehler: page 8
Bobbie Kalman: pages 7 (bottom), 18
The National Audubon Society Collection/Photo Researchers:
  Jean-Phillipe Varin Jacana: page 10; Tom McHugh: page 11
Tom Stack & Associates: Dominique Braud: page 25; E.P.I. Nancy Adams:
  pages 30 (top left), 31 (left); David Fleetham: page 28; Joe McDonald:
  page 22; Thomas Kitchin: page 30 (top right); Gary Milburn:
  pages 30 (bottom), 31 (right); Brian Parker: page 16; Bob Pool:
  page 24 (right); Wendy Shatil/Bob Rozinski: page 19; Roy Toft: page 27
Dave Taylor: page 9
Other photographs by Digital Stock and Digital Vision

Illustrations
Barbara Bedell: pages 5, 10, 13, 16, 18, 19, 20, 23, 24, 25, 28, 29, 31
Jeannette R. Julich: page 27

Printer
Worzalla Publishing Company

Color separations and film
Dot 'n Line Image Inc.
CCS Princeton (cover)

Crabtree Publishing Company

350 Fifth Avenue	360 York Road, RR 4,	73 Lime Walk
Suite 3308	Niagara-on-the-Lake,	Headington
New York	Ontario, Canada	Oxford OX3 7AD
N.Y. 10118	L0S 1J0	United Kingdom

Cataloging in Publication Data
Kalman, Bobbie
    What is a mammal?

(The science of living things)
Includes index.

ISBN 0-86505-878-4 (library bound) ISBN 0-86505-890-3 (pbk.)
This book introduces mammals, showing and describing the main groups
and discussing their anatomy, habitats, reproduction, and diet.

1. Mammals—Juvenile literature. [1. Mammals.] I. Title. II. Series: Kalman,
Bobbie. Science of living things.

QL706.2.K35 1997   j599   LC 97-39884
                                                                  CIP

Contents

What is a mammal?

A mammal is a type of animal. Animals are living things that eat plants or other animals. Mammals are **warm-blooded**, which means their body stays the same temperature no matter how warm or cold their surroundings are. Mammals have hair or fur on their body. In order to stay alive, they need to breathe in oxygen and breathe out carbon dioxide. Mammal mothers are the only animals that feed their babies with milk from their body.

*The animals and children on these two pages are mammals. There are thousands of other kinds. Mammals live all over the world in many types of **habitats**, or natural homes. Some, such as the orca above, live in water. Others, such as the tiger on the right, live on land.*

Groups of mammals

This page shows most of the main groups to which mammals belong. You will learn more about these groups in this book.

platypus

Monotremes lay eggs.

koala

Most **marsupials** have a pouch to hold their babies.

dormouse

Rodents have long teeth for gnawing.

mandrill

Primates have hands and a large brain.

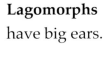
arctic hare

Lagomorphs have big ears.

caracal

Carnivores eat meat.

greater horseshoe bat

Bats can fly.

desert hedgehog

Insectivores eat mainly insects.

dromedary camel

Artiodactyls have hoofs with two or four toes.

white rhinoceros

Perissodactyls have hoofs with one or three toes.

nine-banded armadillo

Edentates have no real teeth.

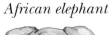
African elephant

Elephants have a long trunk.

manatee

Sirenians eat plants and live in the water.

orca

Cetaceans live in the water. Some hunt other animals for food.

A mammal's body

Mammals have some of the same body parts as other animals but, in many ways, their bodies are special. The pictures on these pages show the most important body parts of mammals.

A mammal's **brain** is bigger than that of any other animal. The brain tells muscles when and how to move. It also controls the animal's nerves and senses.

The **skull** and **jaw** are bones in a mammal's head. The skull protects the brain, and the jaw grabs and chews food.

A mammal's **senses** of sight, hearing, taste, smell, and touch help it find food and avoid danger.

Most mammals have four **limbs** that they use for running, swimming, digging, or holding things.

Lungs bring fresh air into the body. The **heart** pumps blood throughout the body.

A **skeleton** made of bones gives strength and shape to a mammal's body.

Most mammals have a coat of hair or fur that protects their skin.

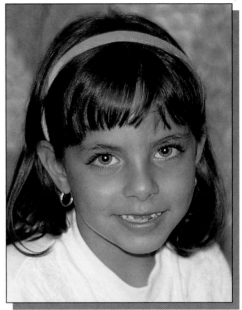

*Young mammals lose their first set of teeth, called **milk teeth**. Larger **permanent teeth** grow in their place.*

Many mammals have a tail. Tails help them swim, grip things, keep their balance, or brush away insects.

*Most mammals breathe through a nose or snout. Dolphins and whales breathe through a **blowhole**.*

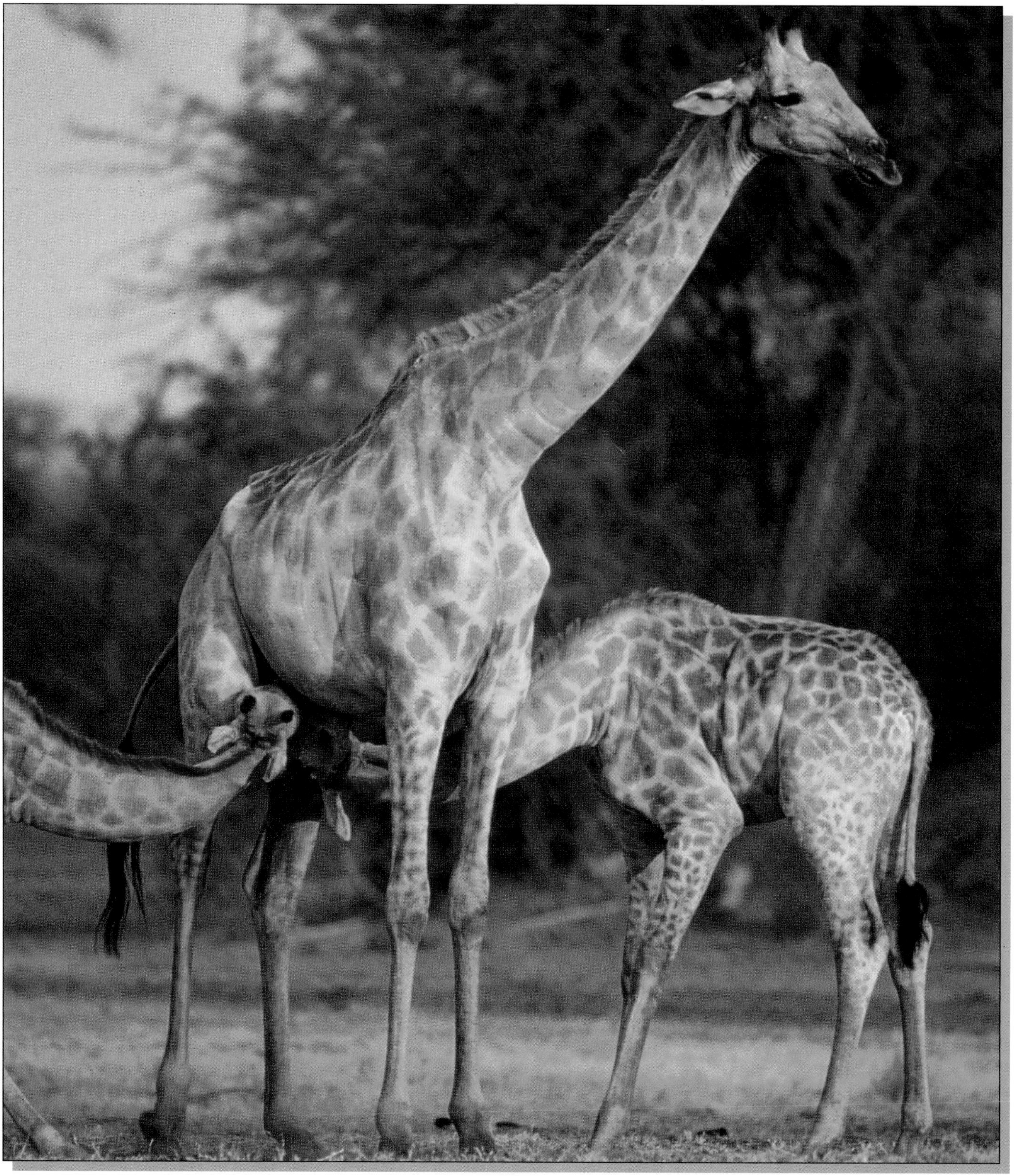

Mammals' milk

Mammal babies are the only animals that are fed milk from their mother's body. Other types of baby animals, such as birds, reptiles, and fish, eat foods like insects and worms right after they are born.

Mammary glands

Milk is made in a female mammal's **mammary glands**. A gland is a body part that makes a liquid. Milk begins flowing from a female mammal's body as soon as she gives birth to a baby. It leaves her body through **nipples** or **teats**, which are at the end of her mammary glands. The nipples or teats easily fit into the baby's mouth.

Nursing

A mother's body keeps making milk as long as her baby keeps **nursing**, or drinking it. As babies grow, they nurse less often and begin to eat the same kinds of foods as their parents. This process is called **weaning**. The babies of different species nurse for different lengths of time. Puppies, for example, nurse about 6 weeks, whereas elephants nurse for two years.

- The female baboon above is feeding her baby. Some mothers with only one baby sit upright and hold it in their arms to feed it.
- Mothers with several babies, called a **litter**, lie on their side so that all the babies can reach a teat and drink at the same time.
- Some mammals, such as horses, cows, and giraffes (shown on the opposite page) nurse their babies standing up. These mammals have a pouch, called an **udder**, that hangs between their hind legs. The teats are at the bottom of the udder.

Monotremes

Monotremes are the only mammals that lay eggs. There are three species of monotremes—the platypus, the short-nosed echidna, and the long-nosed echidna. All monotremes live in Australia and small nearby islands.

The platypus

Platypuses live in underground burrows. They spend a lot of time in rivers looking for food. Platypuses have webbed feet for swimming, and their paddle-like tail helps them steer. With their special nose, they hunt for worms and other small water animals. Their nose can feel the tiny electrical charges given off by prey.

Platypuses get together only when it is time to **breed**. The female lays her eggs and holds them between her tail and belly to keep them warm.

←— spur

*(above) The male platypus is one of the few poisonous mammals. It has a sharp claw called a **spur** on its back paws. The spur is attached to a venom sac inside the platypus's body.*

(right) Unlike other mammals, monotremes have no nipples. Milk oozes from openings on a mother's belly. Her babies lap the milk from her fur.

Echidnas

Both long-nosed and short-nosed echidnas live alone in a burrow. Short-nosed echidnas eat ants and termites. Long-nosed echidnas eat insects and worms. Echidnas sniff out prey with their long snout and dig it up with their sharp claws. Unlike most mammals, echidnas have no teeth. They catch and eat prey with their sticky tongue.

When echidnas are threatened by enemies such as dingoes, foxes, or wild cats, they use their powerful paws and claws to burrow into the ground. They are such good burrowers that, in less than one minute, only the sharp spines on their back remain above the surface.

Female echidnas have a pouch on their body in which they hide their egg and keep it warm until it hatches.

Marsupials

*Most kangaroos have a baby, called a **joey**, growing inside their pouch even while an older joey climbs in and out for milk and protection.*

Marsupials are mammals that give birth to **live young**, or babies that do not hatch from eggs. Koalas, wallabies, wombats, kangaroos, and opossums are some marsupials. There are over 250 species of marsupials. They vary in size and shape. Some live alone, and others live in groups. Most marsupials sleep during the day. They are active from dusk to dawn.

Pouch potatoes

Most female marsupials have a pouch on the outside of their body. When a marsupial is born, it is not fully developed. It is tiny, has no fur, and cannot hear or see. It crawls across its mother's body and into her pouch. While inside, the baby drinks her milk and grows bigger and stronger. Many months pass before the baby has grown enough to leave the safety of its mother's pouch.

Different pouches

Not all marsupial pouches are the same. Kangaroos and possums have pouches that open toward their head. Their baby has farther to travel to reach the opening than the babies of other marsupials such as wombats and koalas. These marsupials have pouches that open toward the rear.

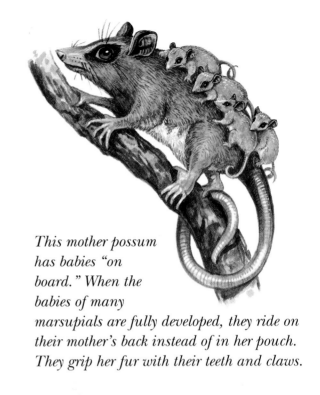

This mother possum has babies "on board." When the babies of many marsupials are fully developed, they ride on their mother's back instead of in her pouch. They grip her fur with their teeth and claws.

Inside its mother's pouch, a baby marsupial such as this kangaroo joey attaches its mouth to one of its mother's nipples. Nourishing milk comes out of the nipple and helps the baby grow.

After six months, a baby koala leaves its mother's pouch for the first time. While outside the pouch, it clings to her back or chest.

Growing with a placenta

Most mammals belong to a group called placentals. Female placentals give birth to live young. Unlike marsupial babies, however, placental babies are well developed when they are born. Some can stand and walk just a few hours after birth.

The name placental comes from the word **placenta**. A placenta is an organ that grows along with a baby inside a placental mother's body. It passes nutrients from the mother's body to the baby. It also passes wastes from the baby to its mother.

Most mammals are placentals

Placental mammals are all shapes and sizes. The mammals on the following pages are placentals. They include primates, rodents, lagomorphs, carnivores, insectivores, bats, artiodactyls, perissodactyls, elephants, edentates, sirenians, and cetaceans.

(above) Elephant mothers are pregnant longer than any other mammal. They carry their baby inside their body for almost two years before it is born!

(opposite) A baby giraffe is helpless seconds after its birth. In only a few hours, however, the baby can stand, walk, and drink its mother's milk.

Primates

There are more than 200 species of primates. Humans, monkeys, gorillas, and lemurs are just a few. Primates are mammals with special hands.

Opposable thumbs

A primate's hand, such as the gorilla's hand below, has four fingers and a thumb. The thumb is **opposable**, which means it can be moved opposite to the fingers. Opposable thumbs allow primates to grip objects tightly in one hand. Mammals that have paws do not have a thumb and cannot grip anything.

Apes are primates that have no tail. This orangutan and its baby are apes. They live on the ground.

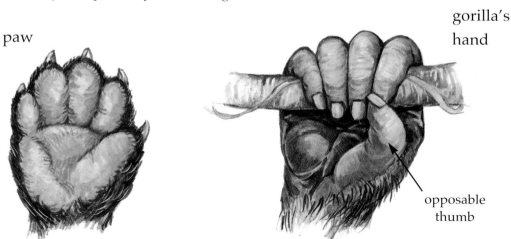

paw

gorilla's hand

opposable thumb

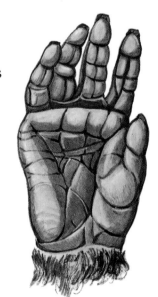

Big brains

A primate's large brain helps it learn quickly. It also allows the primate to use sounds and signs to communicate. Of all the primates, humans have the largest brain.

*(above) Unlike apes, **monkeys** have a tail. Monkeys use their tail to grasp things and keep their balance while climbing trees.*

(right) Lemurs are primates with a bushy tail and a narrow snout. They are the size of a cat and spend their time in trees.

Rodents

Rodents are mammals with long, sharp front teeth. They use them to gnaw through things such as wood or the shells of seeds and nuts. Chewing such hard things wears down teeth but, unlike most other mammals, a rodent's teeth never stop growing. A rodent must keep grinding down its teeth, or they will become so long that its jaw will lock shut.

(below) Most rodents, such as this prairie dog, hold food between their front paws as they chew.

Many kinds of rodents

There are over 1,700 species of rodents, including types of mice, rats, squirrels, beavers, and porcupines. They range in size from the pygmy jerboa, which is under 2 inches (5 cm) long to the capybara, which is over 4 feet (120 cm) long.

Rodent homes

Rodents are found in many habitats all over the world. Some live in nests built under rocks or in hollow logs. Others, such as gophers, chipmunks, and prairie dogs, live underground in burrows joined by tunnels. Many types of squirrels live in holes in trees. Beavers and muskrats are two types of rodents that swim in the water to look for food.

Lagomorphs

Rabbits, hares, and pikas are **lagomorphs**. There are about 60 species. Like rodents, lagomorphs have long front teeth for chewing grasses, leaves, and bark. Unlike rodents, they have very large ears that help heat escape from their body. Their eyes are set high on the sides of their head to spot danger. A lagomorph's long, strong hind legs help it hop to safety. Lagomorphs are eaten by many kinds of animals, and a quick escape is their best defense.

Underground protection

Pikas are found in areas of western North America and northwest Asia. Some live in nests built in crevices, and others live in underground burrows. Rabbits and hares live on almost every continent and in most habitats. Rabbits live in underground burrows, which help them hide from enemies. They dig several burrows that are connected by tunnels. Hares live in nests on the ground and rely on their speed to escape from their enemies.

*Pikas, like rabbits, hares, and rodents, eat some of their own droppings, or **pellets**. Their stomach does not get all the nutrients from food the first time it passes through their body.*

Carnivores

The giant panda feeds mainly on the bamboo plant. It has a special bone in its paw to help grasp and strip bamboo shoots.

*When they are not hunting, hyenas and some other carnivores get food by **scavenging**. They wait for other hunters to make a kill and then move in to steal a meal from the carcass.*

Most people think carnivores are animals that eat only meat. In the carnivore group, however, scientists include many mammals that do not eat just meat. These animals all share common ancestors. The more than 200 species of carnivores look different from one another, but most have two long, pointed front teeth and sharp claws. They are found everywhere in the world. Cats, dogs, bears, wolves, raccoons, and seals are a few examples of carnivores.

The hunters

Some carnivores, such as lions, tigers, and other big cats, are excellent hunters that eat mainly meat. They have keen senses for tracking other animals and use speed to catch them. Sharp teeth and claws help these carnivores easily hold prey and tear flesh.

More than meat

Most carnivores, including foxes, coyotes, bears, weasels, and skunks, eat both plants and meat. Some prefer to eat meat but will eat fruits, berries, or nuts when their usual prey is scarce.

Hunting underwater

Some carnivores have special bodies for hunting in the water. Walruses, sea lions, and seals have flippers instead of paws. Flippers are more useful for swimming. When they are not busy hunting fish, squid, and other creatures in the water, marine carnivores rest on the shore.

A carnivore's pointed teeth help hold prey firmly and can even puncture skin. The sharp teeth in the back of a lion's mouth cut through flesh like a pair of scissors.

(above) Many scientists think that walruses, seals, and sea lions are carnivores. Others put them into their own group.

(right) When they feel threatened, badgers and some other carnivores bare their teeth to warn other animals to back off.

Insectivores

Insectivores eat mainly insects, but some also eat small birds and amphibians. Moles, hedgehogs, and shrews are some types of insectivores. There are about 400 species. Most are **nocturnal**, which means they are active at night. Insectivores live on every continent except Australia and Antarctica.

Most insectivores have a long, thin snout that they use to sniff for prey in crevices and underground. They have excellent hearing, but their eyes are small because sight is not useful for hunting in these dark places. Most have short, powerful legs that quickly dig through leaves and dirt to reach hidden prey.

The single life

Almost all insectivores are **solitary**, which means they live alone. They inhabit a variety of homes. Moles live in burrows and spend most of their life tunneling underground. Some shrews move into a mole's burrow after it has been abandoned. Others live in nests built on forest floors. A few types live near rivers and streams, where they dive for food. Hedgehogs, such as the one on the left, live in nests on the ground.

Bats

Bats, or **chiropterans**, are the only mammals that can fly. Bats fly by constantly flapping their leathery wings. Bats cannot glide as birds can.

Fruit, meat, and blood

Bats look for food at dusk, dawn, or nighttime. There are two main groups of bats. One group eats mostly fruit. These bats have large eyes to see where they are going and to find food. More than 800 species belong to the second group of bats. These bats are hunters that feed mainly on insects. A few eat fish, mice, and birds. The vampire bat feeds only on the blood of large animals such as cows, pigs, and horses.

Echolocation

Bats that hunt do not see well, but they have an excellent sense of hearing. They use **echolocation** to find their way and to hunt. They send out sounds that bounce off an object and back to the bats' ears, letting the bat know the position of that object.

(left) This bat spots food with its large eyes.
(top) The horseshoe bat uses echolocation.

Perissodactyls

Horses, tapirs, and rhinos are perissodactyls. Perissodactyls are mammals with **hoofs**. A hoof is a hard covering on the bottom of a foot. It protects the feet and toes of these mammals when they run. Perissodactyls are **odd-toed**, which means they have one or three toes on each foot.

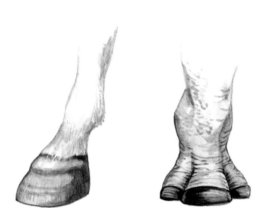

A horse or zebra has one toe. A rhinoceros has three.

Grasslands, farms, and forests

Rhinoceroses and tapirs live alone. Tapirs are found in the forests of South America and Asia. Rhinos live in parts of Africa and Asia. Wild horses live in herds on the grasslands of North America, Australia, and southwest Asia.

The rhinoceros is the only perissodactyl that grows horns.

Humans use horses as work animals and have taken them all over the world.

Artiodactyls

Giraffes, deer, pigs, camels, sheep, cows, and hippos are all artiodactyls. These animals have hoofs with two or four toes on each foot. They are **even-toed**. All artiodactyls are hunted by meat-eating animals. Their feet are well designed for quick getaways. Their hoofs provide excellent traction for running.

On land and in water

Artiodactyls are **herbivores**, or plant-eaters, that wander in search of leaves and grass to eat. They can be found in forests, grasslands, shrublands, and on mountains. The hippopotamus is the only artiodactyl that lives in the water during the day and comes out at night to feed.

Special stomachs

Many kinds of artiodactyls, such as cows and giraffes, have a special stomach that helps break down the tough grasses and leaves eaten by these animals. The stomach changes the food into soft balls of **cud**. The animal coughs up the cud, rechews it, and then swallows it again.

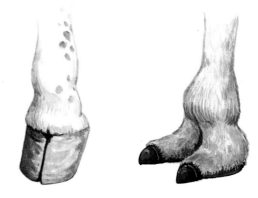

An antelope's foot is split into two toes. A camel's foot has two broad toes that keep its foot from sinking in sand.

Camels have one or two humps for storing fat. Their body uses the fat when there is little food.

Elephants

Scientists call elephants **proboscideans.** There are only two species—the African and the Asian elephants. Elephants are the largest land animals. Their body can be 13 feet (4 m) long, and their trunk can be over 6 1/2 feet (2 m) long.

The useful trunk

Elephants have a long, flexible nose and upper lip called a **trunk**. With its trunk, an elephant can pick up food and water to put into its mouth. It can gently touch its mate or babies. An elephant also uses its trunk to communicate with others by trumpeting and making deep, rumbling sounds.

In search of food

Elephants eat grasses, leaves, bark, fruit, and flowers. They do not have permanent homes. They wander in search of food. Females and their babies usually travel in herds. Males live alone or in small herds.

An elephant's trunk reaches food high off the ground.

Scientists think that the elephant's closest relatives are sirenians (page 28), the hyrax, and the aardvark (both on page 30).

Edentates

Sloths, anteaters, and armadillos are edentates. Edentate means "toothless." This name is misleading because anteaters are the only ones that are toothless. All edentates have strong, curved claws. Sloths use their long claws to hang onto tree branches, where they spend their time eating leaves and sleeping. Anteaters and armadillos use their claws for digging.

Lone dwellers

Edentates live alone. The armadillo and giant anteater rest in a burrow during the day. At night, they roam forests and grasslands in search of food. Armadillos eat insects, roots, and small animals. Giant anteaters eat ants and termites. Other species of anteaters eat only ants. These anteaters, like sloths, live in trees.

*Sloths are the slowest-moving mammals. They move so slowly that tiny, green plants called **algae** grow on their fur!*

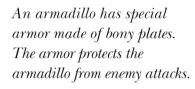

An armadillo has special armor made of bony plates. The armor protects the armadillo from enemy attacks.

Sirenians

Sirenians are mammals that live underwater and eat plants. There are only four species of sirenians—three are manatees and the other is the dugong. They are all about 10 feet (2.5 m) long.

Sometimes mother manatees hold their baby. (top) Dugongs use their front flippers to swim and to dig up plant roots for food.

Life on the coast

To feed on seaweed and other water plants, sirenians must stay in shallow waters. Manatees live in fresh and salt waters along the coasts of Florida, the Caribbean, and the northern coast of South America. Dugongs live along the coasts of eastern Africa, the Philippines, and northern Australia.

Swimming and breathing

Manatees and dugongs are good swimmers. Their long, almost hairless body slips through water easily. Each sirenian has two flippers and a flat tail that help it swim. When a manatee or dugong needs air, it pokes its head above the surface and breathes through its nostrils.

Cetaceans

blue whale

Cetaceans are dolphins and whales. There are about about 80 species of these mammals. Some are over 100 feet (30m) long. The blue whale is the largest animal that has ever lived!

Their underwater world

Like sirenians, cetaceans spend their whole life in the water. They live in all the oceans, and a few species are found in rivers. They have smooth skin, a flat tail, and flippers for swimming.

They have a **blowhole** on top of their head through which they breathe when they surface for air. Cetaceans often live in groups called **schools**.

Toothed and baleen whales

There are two main groups of cetaceans. **Toothed whales** have teeth and hunt other animals for food. **Baleen whales**, such as the blue whale, have no teeth, and filter bits of food from the water.

*Dolphins are toothed whales. This dolphin is **porpoising**, or leaping from the water while moving quickly.*

Other mammals

There are several placental mammals that do not belong to any of the groups already mentioned in this book.

Tree shrews

There are nineteen species of tree shrews. They are found in Asia and northern Australia. Most tree shrews live in trees, but some live on the ground. They have a lot of sharp teeth for eating insects and lizards. Some scientists think that tree shrews belong in their own group, but others think they are primates or insectivores.

Hyraxes

There are four species of hyraxes. These mammals have special foot pads that help them grip rocks as they climb. They eat plants and live together in trees in dry, rocky areas of Africa and Asia.

Aardvarks

The one species of aardvark lives in Africa. Aardvarks dig up insects with their claws and catch them on their sticky tongue. They live alone, hunting at night and resting in their burrow during the day.

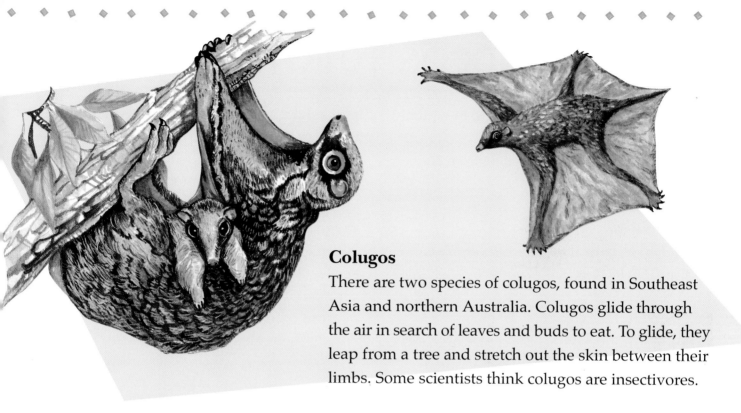

Colugos

There are two species of colugos, found in Southeast Asia and northern Australia. Colugos glide through the air in search of leaves and buds to eat. To glide, they leap from a tree and stretch out the skin between their limbs. Some scientists think colugos are insectivores.

Pangolins

The seven species of pangolins live on the ground and in trees in Africa, Asia, and northern Australia. They are the only mammals covered with scales. Pangolins catch insects on their sticky tongue, which is almost as long as their body!

Elephant shrews

The fourteen species of elephant shrews use their flexible snout to sniff out insects, seeds, and fruit. They live on the ground in Africa. Some scientists think they are insectivores.

Words to know

burrow A hole dug in the ground in which an animal lives or hides

claws The sharp, often curved nails on an animal's paws

communicate To deliver a message to another creature

habitat The natural place where a plant or animal is found

herd A group of plant-eating animals that live together

nipple A rounded tip at the center of a breast or udder through which a baby mammal drinks milk

placental Describing a mammal that, before it is born, grows inside its mother's body along with an organ called a placenta

predator An animal that kills and eats other animals

pregnant Describing a female animal that has one or more babies growing inside her

senses The abilities that help an animal be aware of its surroundings, including sight, hearing, smell, taste, and touch

snout The nose and mouth of an animal

species A group of very similar living things whose offspring can reproduce

Index

1 2 3 4 5 6 7 8 9 0   Printed in the U.S.A.   6 5 4 3 2 1 0 9 8 7